Mustelus canis

Zachary Webb Nicholls

I0116359

The sale of this book without a front cover is unauthorized. If this book is sold without a cover, then the author and the publishing company may have not received payment for it.

Mustelus canis

Copyright © 2016 by Zachary Webb Nicholls (a.k.a Dr. Jaws)

All rights reserved. Published in the United States by Deep Sea Publishing LLC, Herndon, Virginia.

This is a work of fiction. Names, characters, places, and incidents either are the product of the author's imagination or are used fictionally. Any resemblance to actual persons, living or dead, events or locales is entirely coincidental.

ISBN-13: 978-1-939535-90-0
ISBN: 1939535905
E-Book ISBN-13: 978-1-939535-91-7
E-Book ISBN: 1939535913

www.deepseapublishing.com

Printed in the United States of America

Hello friend,

What you are about to read is secret.

Each word, picture, and symbol has a meaning, and together they will help you find something very strange, but very exciting. Furthermore, each word, picture, and symbol is anchored in a living truth, but in order to fully understand what that truth is, you need to do some exploring.

Beyond this little book, there is a boundless, bountiful wealth of knowledge within your reach. You of course are not required to seek it, but if you do, I assure you will be rewarded with a richer understanding of our shark, the seas, and the mystery of life itself.

For now, you hold in your hands a map. Let it take you—from the past, to the present, to the weird—deep into an ocean of legends, of dark wonders, and of amber eyes…

….let it take you to Shark.

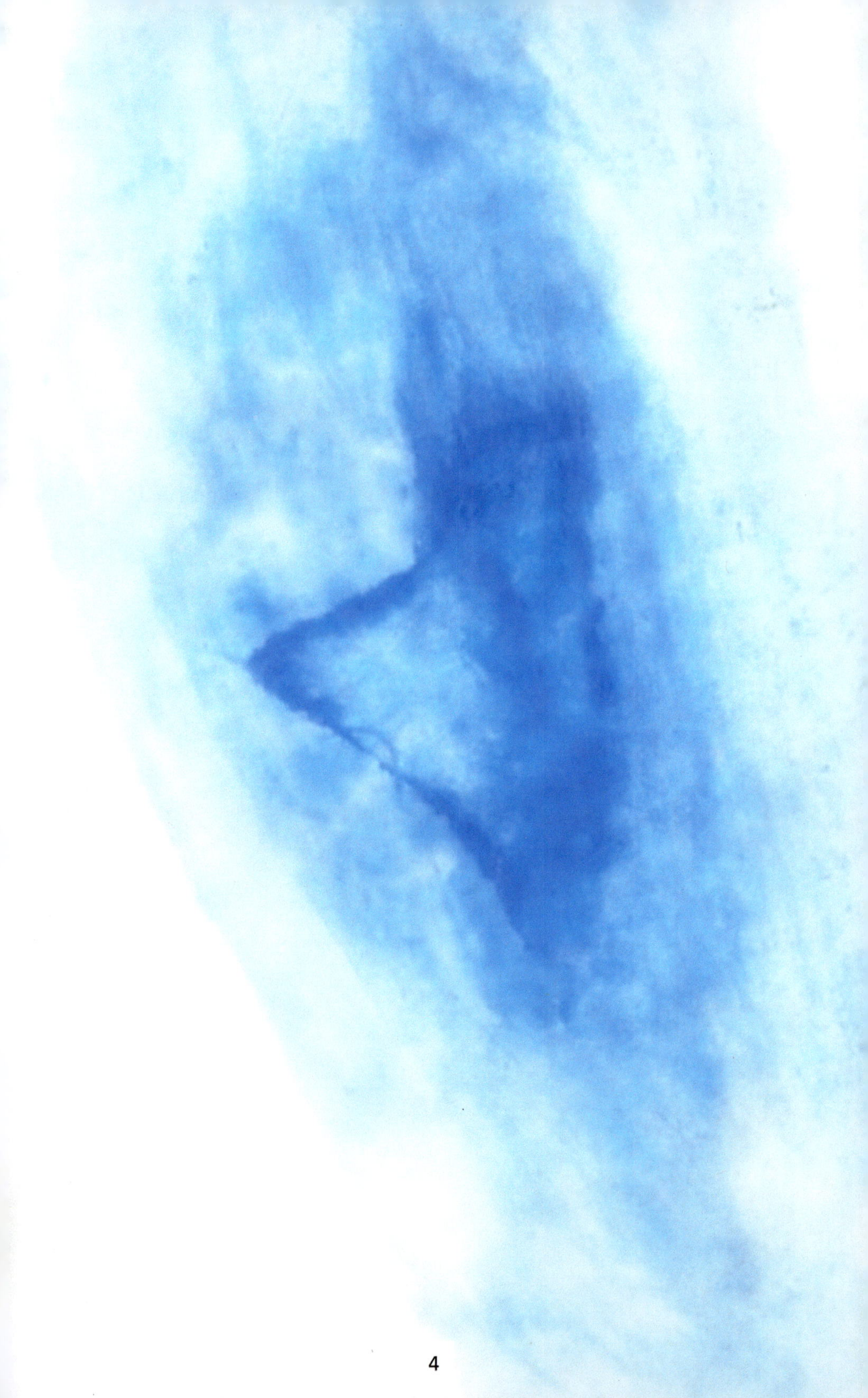

Beneath the isle wide

Amongst a full moon tide

Where softest lights abide

I reside, I reside

With vision clear and wide

And colors mirroring tide

Where masquerades abide

I reside, I reside

Starlight is finite
A star has a time to end
Explosive its death

Scattered star pieces
Combine into the combined
Birth of sun and earth

Sun fire creates
With calm earth, air, and
water
Life elemental

~ *Domain Eukarya* ~

Imagine a mountain

Cool and calming

Trickling water down its slope

It is serene in its grey

Paint it with a domain

Of life so rich in color

That the eyes will forever wonder

At its design and sustain

A curiosity

Unique only to Eukarya

When cell within cell became cell itself

So long ago, a peak

In life was reached

From origins so humble

Came oranges so fiery

With jades, emeralds, and harlequins each

Beauties of the forest

Protecting the ambling reds

And boisterous blues

With calming arms best

Suited for shading

Amber-centered violets

And cinnabar-sighted mosaics

All art never fading

This domain is of color

See Eukarya

Splendid and diverse

Muses of the world

For the art that it is

~Kingdom Animalia~

Look what the dawn has broken

Something new stirs in the seas

A novel language now spoken

The animals have come to be

~

From one tiny sponge to one funny man

A simple life will always be banned

A drama that we cannot understand

The animals, come and play, come and play

A hardworking ant meets an unfriendly beetle

While two birds romance, it seems nothing's sweeter

A seahorse's dance is such a unique love

Animals, come and play, come and play

~

Embrace the feeling of life

A body that's one from many

A hunger that sets you right

~

And chase in manner uncanny

Your strange sweet compassions

You animal, go and play, go and play

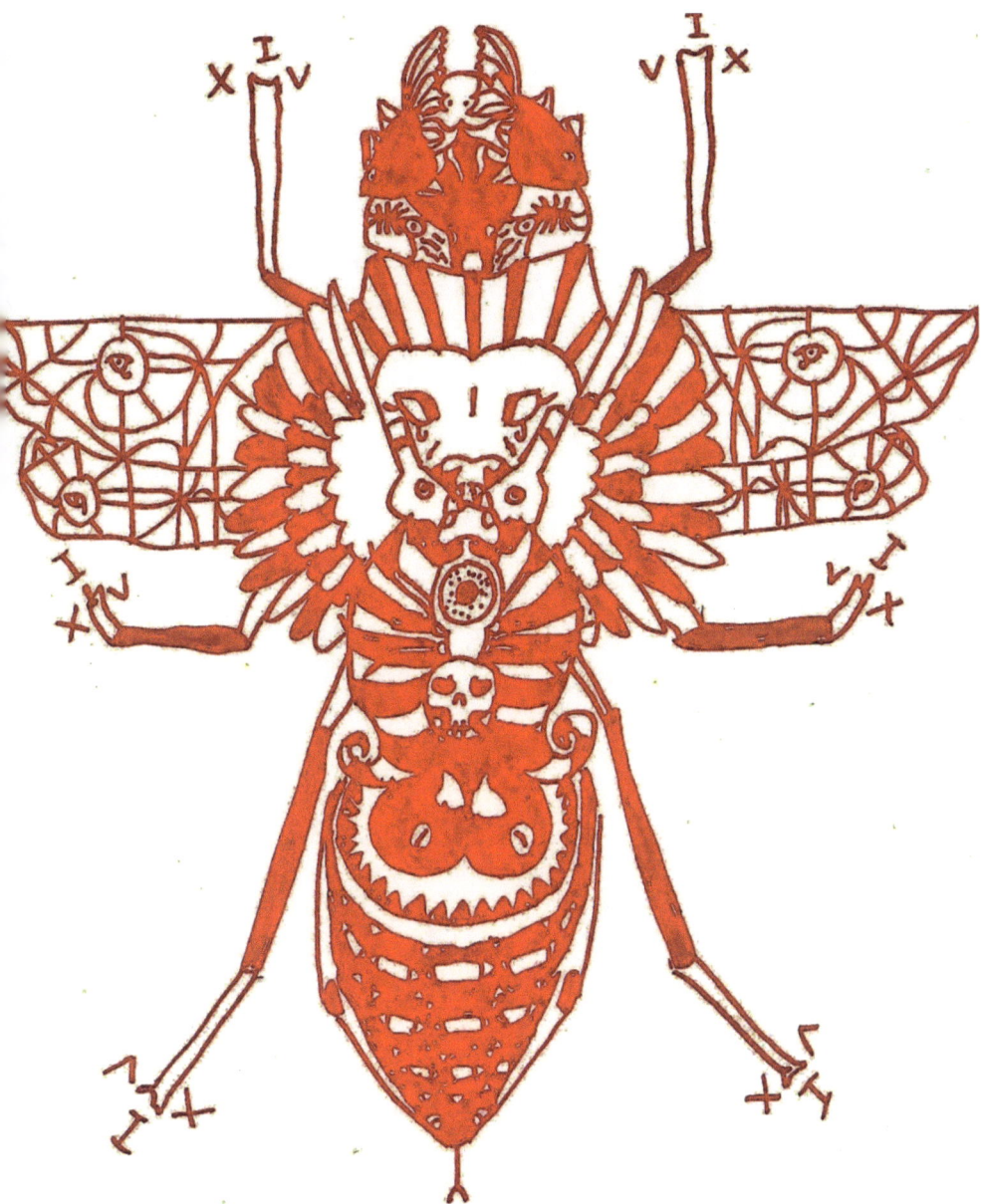

~Phylum Chordata~

CORD

now is the time to change the organism

SISTERS

Brothers

we are related

but we are... h...

NOT

BILATERALS

we are unalike

IN VIEW

NOTOCHORD

CONG...

in the HCE in

form... OHR... style

ROVa

DRE!

tion

D

tail...

~ *Class Chondrichthyes* ~

There is a hall of marble and limestone—of honor and ocean—adorned with obsidian shadows; the Chondrichthyan Silhouettes. Each Silhouette is an embodiment of form and essence, said to be constructed by the gods to remind the world of the Living Shadows; the chimaera, the ray, and the shark. Believed to be guardians of both the ocean and the human soul, The Living Shadows served to consume the weaknesses of each. Through so doing, they culled corruption and pro- tected the life of both soul and sea. To honor this nobility cloaked in ferocity, the Chondrichthyan Silhouettes are each adorned with an eye of pearl and gemstone. Together, body and eye capture the essence of a Living Shadow:

A power cooled with grace
An immortal who could die
A legend with a heartbeat.

15

~Order Carcharhiniformes~

Beauteous beasts of time
A standard and yet an ideal
Coasting beyond the sands
And into depths of teal

For fear they do not
As in their eyes reveal
An ancient secret light
Seen only by those who feel

Akin to their plight
And akin to their strength
A cutting edge of blue
A coursing blood of length

By such eyes as theirs
Which close upon a kill
They form their sacred forms
The fears that we've instilled

These rare and common types
Of shark will always be
As changing as the tides
But still masters of the sea

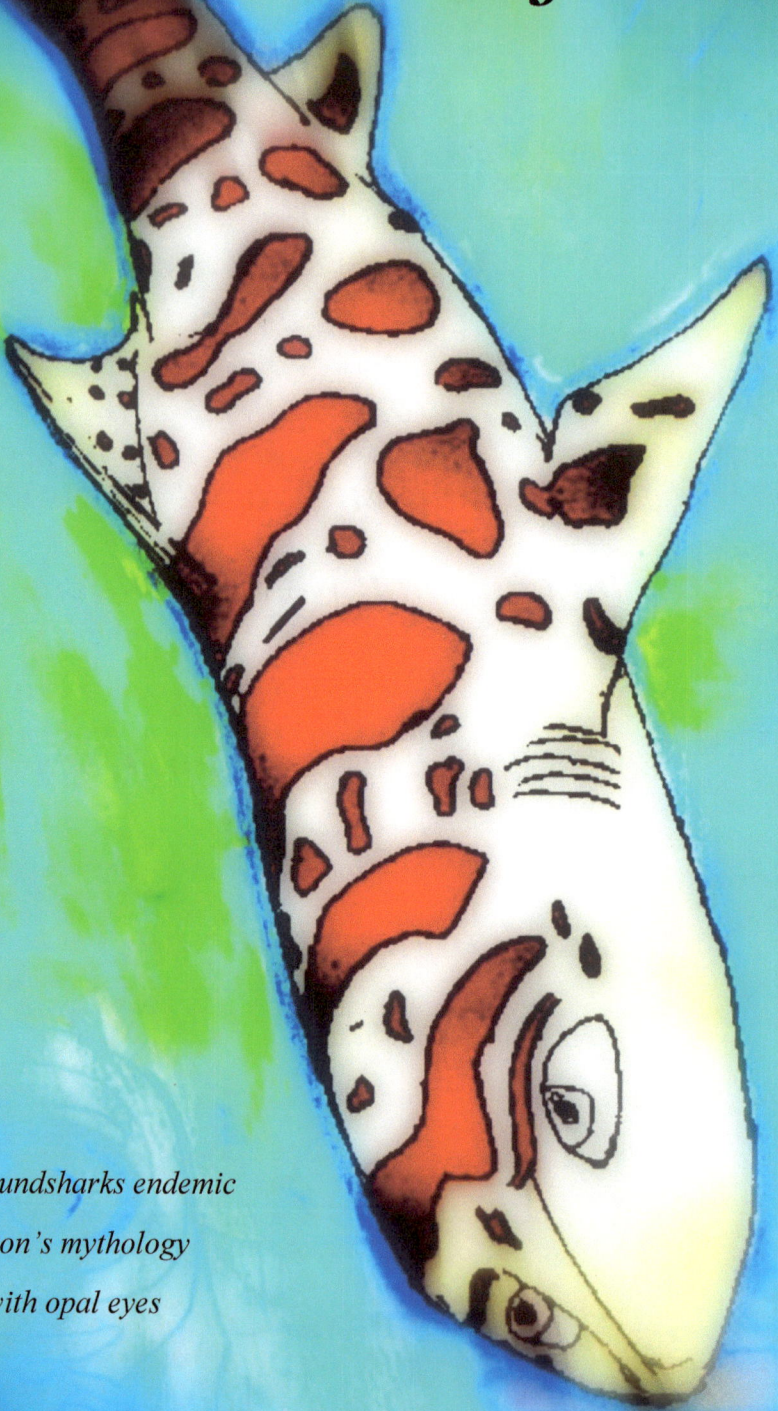

~Family Triakidae~

The houndsharks endemic
To Triton's mythology
Gaze with opal eyes

~*Genus Mustelus*~

WEASEL

"Sbhrh hghamks hqjdkhr dkrodqh m Aqhhf jnsdl; sbhdq vhqy jnvhjhks dr qhjdkdrthks nl nkgy sbh mktdhks mqsr"

Note: The above is a keyword cypher. The keyword is hidden on the following page. Use it to unlock a smaller insight.

The Dog

Mitchill, 1815

Mustelus canis

A tiny shark with an average mass of 3kg. It is distinguished by its slender body, flat pavemental teeth, and rounded lower caudal lobe.

Dusky Smoothhound   Viuda dientuda

كلب البحــر الأملـس النَّاعم   美星鲨   イヌホシザ

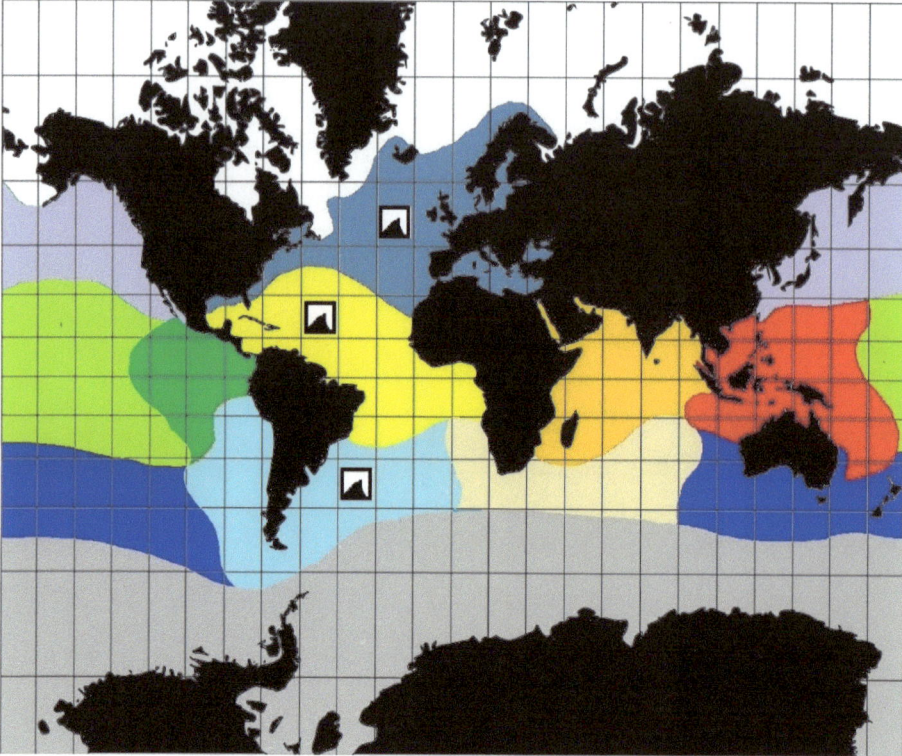

~Global Distribution~

North Akula Sea

Tempest Requin Sea ◢

Wild Zame Sea

Sunset Sea of Reken ◢

Colorful Sea of Sarka

Bountiful Sea of Shayu

Peaceful Sea of Mano

Sunrise Sea of Tiburon

Grande Tubarao Sea ◢

Groot Haai Sea

Great Shark Sea

South Sarko Sea

~Haunts~

Mustelus canis

can be found in the following zones:

Littoral   **Neritic**

Sunlit   **Twilight**

~

"We cannot reveal who we are…not directly at least…but perhaps you can observe—be you keen of eye—the telling clues to our design."

~ *Habits* ~

Mustelus canis is able to change skin color to better camouflage itself with the seabed. The color-change is accomplished through the contraction of melanophores (dark pigments in cells). Very few sharks possess this talent.

Mustelus canis is also unique in its dentition; the shark's teeth are small, flat, and arranged in a pavement designed ideally for crushing shellfish. Crabs are a particular favorite for this active smoothhound shark.

~ *Humanity* ~

Mustelus canis is to be perceived as a

HARMLESS SHARK

In light of the comforting attributes that follow;

Its tiny size

Its flattened dentition

These attributes are presented with the truth that
Mustelus canis has been implicated in

NO ATTACKS WHATSOEVER

As a resource, the shark offers palatable meat and is a
popular focus of both public aquaria and laboratory
studies

~

However, man has threatened *Mustelus canis* with
gillnet and longline fishing in spite of the species' rather
quick rate of reproduction.

As a result, *Mustelus canis* is a

SUSCEPTIBLE SPECIES

~ *Full Moon Isle* ~

"A tale about our shark, and yet much more..."

Night is where you found me...I echo throughout the night...

Welcome to Full Moon Isle. You are standing alone in a darkness ignited by the galaxy; the stars seem to favor your presence, and will tend to your wanderings. Indeed you must wander…for there is so much to see.

Firstly, the Isle, though abandoned, is not lonely. Far from it, this place is a comfort; a small patch of dusky grass perched atop Acadian boulders and crags constantly pummeled by the sea. The Isle is roughly circular and with little feature, save for an abandoned seafarer's cabin behind you. But you don't want to go there.

You want to move forward…there's a jetty of dark boulders climbing towards the moonlight. Quickly, run to it! Feel the wind fall behind you, and be carried by the wings of enticement. Your curiosity must be slaked, for you believe there is something beyond the rocks.

The full moon is massive, and starting to set. You must get closer.

Swiftly, you come across a change in terrain; the grass stops, and pebbles become dominant. Your pace slows; carefully you place your feet into the massaging grip of each patch of stones. Some are beveled, others smooth, some with caramel strips, leopard speckles…eventually their numbers decrease as you approach the larger boulders. These present more of a challenge, as they are closer to the tide; they are slippery, and dangerous, but you don't mind. You rather enjoy scaling them, employing your animal nature…each peak you reach yields a new night horizon, and empowers your will to explore further.

The water begins to take over.

Your feet get wet—cold even—but you still don't mind. The moon is setting, and you must chase it. Finally, the grandest peak of all is before you, and you ascend it with a focus reserved only for Everest. The knotted seaweed serves as traction—a place to grip and become closer to the sea—whilst the barnacles provide an exhilarating danger with their shark-tooth casings. Deftly avoiding them and reaching the top, you behold a wonder.

The entire ocean surrounds not only you, but also a ring of massive sea rocks appearing as pillars of shadow; within the heart of the ring, is a single, perfect pool. Something is curious about this placement.

The moon is falling unnaturally quick…its pace is…deliberate. Passing over you, it arrives at a point almost directly above the face of the pool. At this particular instance, more curiosities emerge; the water tricking from the surrounding rocks begins to glow. Slowly, the illumination penetrates the pool, and something universal immediately changes.

The cosmic is locked.

You.

Need.

To.

Dive.

In.

Without worry, without fear, you leap off of your peak, and approach, with the strongest of gravities, the shimmering mirror of pale moon pool.

T
R
A
N
S
C
E
N
D

Welcome to Full Moon Isle.

You are somewhere beneath the island, but where exactly, you cannot say. A bright, aquamarine portal is above you, and you are completely submerged in a sea without temperature. You may breathe.

Looking around, you feel that this place is not devoid of life. The portal's light illuminates a grand sphere of water surrounded by darkness, and you feel the presence of beings in the shadows.

Slowly, you descend. Very slowly…let yourself sink. There is no rush or hurry in this place…there is no time here.

Softly, you touch the bottom. Though you may feel this to be a surreal circumstance, you observe a very definite seabed composed of the finest grains arranged in the most pleasing of tide-crafted contours. Moonbeams gradually penetrate this arena, and quite literally shed light on the minute particles that abound in the surrounding water. Suddenly, a beam before you offers a quick, magnified glimpse of the finer details of this diminutive matter. In one instance you see an abundance of green cells; some are whirling freely, while others are serving as food for larger, more complex designs. These latter creatures vary greatly in appearance, with either gigantic eyes, elongated spines, or polished claws serving as a their most significant feature.

They are all plankton, the keystones of marine life, and they entice the appetite of millions.

A sudden burst of forage fish—herring, mackerel, and capelin—collides into the sphere. They ignite your eyes with shimmering reflections of the moonlight, and career from edge-to-edge, creating a brilliant orbit of voracious predation. You count seven different schools appearing and disappearing into the darkness; at times when you cannot see them, you still hear an incredibly thunderous chorus of scales breaking the water.

Perhaps also listening to this cacophony, two mantas—one white, one black—elegantly glide into the sphere of light. Each perfectly mirrors the other's flight, and both gently disrupt the seven schools, one-by-one, taking only a small portion of fish as their own claims.

So is the Way.

This dance before you will yield something. The artisans perhaps intended this. Or perhaps this is consequence of the art. In either case, a final school is coming.

You hear it first...a different pattern of scales. More silent, more spectral...a litheness in the water. You feel an electric chill that excites you, but you are still grounded by your reverence. You will be escorted by the otherworldly. Where to, you cannot say.

Enter the shark.

After a final pass between the two mantas, a single, tiny, but commanding shark enters the sphere of light. It approaches from a higher point and descends to meet you, ignoring the colossal globes of fish and the further dances of the rays. Gravely, it wishes to intercept you. Standing taller in understanding of what will be, you accept the arrival.

The shark first drifts towards your head, processing behind amber eyes the secrets you reveal with your own. It then encircles you, periodically moving from an orbit level with your head to one level with your toes. Another appears from an unseen vantage and creates a similar path. A third shark forms a larger circle with your waist as its center. A fourth does the same but sets your heart as its anchor.

Three more sharks join the group, but swim in a pattern much more cryptic than the other four. Their paths seem illogical, but deep within, you understand…

The sphere falls out of focus. The seven sharks forge a new structure of light.

A blue channel ignites within the adjacent darkness, and leads upwards to a high entrance of what appears to be a grotto. The seven sharks immediately swim into the channel, and you follow them with an odd but pleasant emotion; you are playful, but grave, excited, but exposed. You are to follow them…it is the only way.

Upwards you ascend, and soon approach the magnificent rocky entrance to a grotto bathed in aquamarine light. The sharks pass through, and you follow suit.

Leaving the vastness of the arena behind, you find yourself in a much more intimate setting. The grotto begins as a submarine tunnel of bright rocks covered in pink and orange sponges and corals; the occasional crab scuttles here and there, and soft corals gently sway to what subtle current the grotto offers. One of the sharks snaps up a small crab en route to its destination; all seven are just in front of you, whirling upwards in response to oncoming nooks and crags formed by the twisting tunnel. Eventually, the water becomes brighter, more translucent, and the colors more vibrant; you're at a shallower depth.

At this point, the surface is just above you, and you find yourself centered within a modest cavern pool. Somehow, everything is illuminated, though as you break the surface, you spy a definite ceiling. No sunlight.

It is shallow enough to walk, and you head towards a nearby bar of stone. The cavern's walls are handsomely sculpted into a natural atrium, neither too grand nor too claustrophobic in size, but perfectly fitted to your comfort. As you seat yourself upon the limestone bar, you observe behind you a second pool of a deeper turquoise shade. You spy within its waters the faint outlines of carved marble—a rather odd site for a natural cave—and further observe what appears to be a sculpture.

Looking back again to the first pool, you see the sharks preforming a brief survey; they glide smoothly along the rocky edges, passing in front of you once, then twice, and finally a third time. After this final pass, they make a sudden leap.

One-by-one, each shark abruptly launches itself across the bar, escaping the first pool and diving into the second. They seem to disregard you as they fly quickly past your left side, but you feel an intention. You should follow them.

Once the seventh shark has made its leap, you too enter the pool. Slowly the water embraces your back, then head, stomach, legs, and feet, and you are immersed. The pool feeds into a similar tunnel, and the colors fade to an electric blue as you feel yourself sinking deeper. Unlike in your previous encounter, this passage is rather devoid of life, but instead full of strange curios.

More carved blocks of marble…shards in the rubble…a polished cavern wall with…symbols? Effigies…serene faces looking past the walls…to where does this passage lead?

Beneath a final turn of the twisting tunnel, you arrive at a grand hallway. The ceiling is gigantic; the pale walls are smoothed and covered with millions of patterns and symbols, all arranged in a strange grander design. The predominant shapes you see are ellipses. Within each carving are bits of algae and sponge, some in large mats, others in isolated pockets. Life has made a home here.

A fallen statue of an imposing figure—a god perhaps—lies far beneath you. Its head is broken off from its torso, its limbs are severed, and its cuts are many. However, what should be a grotesque sight is actually quite stunning; each of the broken pieces of the god is at rest, comfortably lying between great stones and other fractured fragments of the floor. Sea life covers everything; anemones and corals intersperse between the algae and barnacles, and pairs of spotted butterflyfish drift between small groups of damsels, angels, and idols.

But ahead of you lies the most magnificent sight of all.

A titanic chamber adjoins the hall. In the distance, colossi stand with arms outstretched. The aqua tint of the water fades to something clearer, and you observe above you a ceiling of a billion stars.

The sharks appear to have gone…though you can still feel them…somehow…

What to do?

Do you approach the colossi? Do you ascend to the stars? Should you descend to the depths? Should you go back? Should you explore further?

What are you seeking?

Where did you hope the sharks would take you?

Why are you here?

Suddenly, you notice a star growing larger…wait, it's not a star…it's the moon? Its growing larger because…because it's coming closer! Faster and faster, it falls…towards…

You.

Fearless and focused, you begin your escape. The collision course seems unavoidable, but you dive down anyway. The sheer terror and thrill of the spectacle illuminates you; regardless of who you were before, you now feel the breath of your spirit. The pale light intensifies and you sense the massive rush of pressure loom closer and closer. You are still diving, but you want to be taken. The colossi in the distance, dwarfed by the impacting sphere, begin to fracture, and you feel the water rush out into the heavens. Far below, the seven sharks have made an escape—you know they will be alright—and as they burrow beneath the tiny crags deep below, you feel the icy blaze of pure moonlight…

Wake.

You sit up. You find yourself lying in the middle of a small grassy field. It is night, and you smell a calm sea breeze. You glance left and spy an abandoned seafarer's cabin. You hear waves and other sounds of a nocturnal sea.

Rise.

Welcome to Full Moon Isle. You are standing alone in a darkness ignited by the galaxy; the stars seem to favor your presence, and will tend to your wanderings. Indeed you must wander…for there is so much to see.

Respect the seas and all who call them home.

~ *Thanks* ~

"To my grandmother Patricia Fitzgibbon, who will always love the ocean, the Irish, and the color green.

To Andy Murch, who possesses a plethora of powerful photos at Elasmodiver.com, thank you for your stunning shot of Mustelus canis (page 21). It made all the difference.

To those who may be inspired, never trade your inspiration. You can be whomever you want; that choice is always yours. Always seek to understand yourself, and never let go of your love."

~*Zachary W. Nicholls*
The First Dr. Jaws

www.ingramcontent.com/pod-product-compliance
Lightning Source LLC
Chambersburg PA
CBHW041222270326

41933CB00001B/13